Andrew Tate TopG:

How To Be An Alpha Male That Does Not Give A Fuck

Cobra TopG

Contents

Copyright

Chapter 1

The Journey to Becoming an Alpha Male

1.1 My personal story and the importance of being an alpha male

What's up, losers? It's your boy, Andrew Tate. I'm here to tell you how fed up the world is these days. Men are becoming pussies, broke, and just downright weak. The matrix mindset has got everyone so wrapped up in a bubble that they can't see how pathetic they've become. So I've decided to take matters into my own hands and teach you motherfers how to be a real man, an alpha male.

Let me give you a little backstory about yours truly. I was born into a life of adversity. My father, Emory Andrew Tate II, was a chess Grandmaster and a kickboxing world champion. So, I guess you could say I was bred for greatness. But it wasn't all sunshine and rainbows, my friends. I grew up with racism, poverty, and all kinds of challenges that would break a lesser man. But that's the thing – I ain't no lesser man. I took those challenges, learned from them, and turned them into the fire that fuels me every f***ing day.

You see, being an alpha male isn't just about having muscles or banging hot chicks (although, trust me, that's a pretty sweet perk). It's about rising above the mediocrity that society expects of you. It's about taking control of your own life and destiny, not being a f***ing sheep.

So why is it so important to be an alpha male? Well, for starters, you'll have the respect of your peers, which is something money can't buy. You'll have the power to influence and lead others, and let me tell you, there's no better feeling than being in charge. You'll become the kind of man that other men aspire to be, and the kind of man that women desire. And, of course, you'll never have to settle for being a beta b**** again.

You might think that all of this sounds great, but you're probably also thinking, "Tate, how the f*** do I actually become an alpha male?" Well, that's what this book is for, my friends. I'm going to give you the blueprint to transform yourself from a weak-ass, pathetic excuse for a man into a true alpha male.

Throughout this book, I'll be sharing anecdotes from my own life – the good, the bad, and the ugly. I've been through the ringer, and I've come out the other side stronger, smarter, and more successful than ever. And you can do it too.

We'll cover everything from how to develop a strong mindset to how to fight like a real man. We'll talk about leadership, relationships, and all the things that make an alpha male who he is. By the time you're done with this book, you'll have the tools and knowledge to become the kind of man you've always wanted to be.

But let me warn you – this journey won't be easy. It's going to take blood, sweat, and tears. You'll have to face your demons, confront your weaknesses, and push through your limitations. But I promise you, it'll be worth it. So buckle up, motherf***ers, because it's time to become the alpha male you were always meant to be.

Now, before we dive into the nitty-gritty, let me lay down some ground rules. This book ain't for the faint of heart. If you're easily offended or can't handle some harsh truths, then this ain't the book for you. So, if you're still here, I assume you're ready to get your hands dirty and transform into the badass alpha male you were meant to be.

Let me be clear about something – nobody is born an alpha male. It's not some genetic gift that you either have or don't have. Becoming an alpha male is a f***ing choice. It's a decision you make every day to be better, stronger, and smarter than the weak-ass betas around you. So if you're willing to put in the work, you can become an alpha male, no matter who you are or where you come from.

One of the first things you need to do is to take a long, hard look in the mirror and be brutally honest with yourself. Where are your weaknesses? What are your fears? What's holding you back? You can't fix what you don't acknowledge, so own your s*** and be ready to tackle it head-on.

Next, you need to start building a solid foundation for your new alpha male life. That means getting your body in peak physical condition, learning how to defend yourself, and developing the mental fortitude to face any challenge that comes your way.

Trust me, there's no better feeling than knowing you can handle any situation, whether it's a street fight or a boardroom negotiation.

But being an alpha male isn't just about being a tough guy. It's about understanding the world around you and learning how to navigate it to your advantage. You need to become a master of social dynamics, understanding what makes people tick and how to influence them. You'll need to learn the art of seduction, not just to get laid (although, again, that's a nice perk), but to build powerful relationships that will propel you to greater heights.

In this book, I'll share the lessons I've learned from a life of ups and downs, successes and failures, victories and defeats. I'll tell you the stories of how I built a multi-million dollar business empire, became a world-class kickboxer, and navigated the treacherous waters of the dating scene. I'll give you the inside scoop on the tactics and strategies that have helped me rise above the competition and become the man I am today.

But don't expect me to sugarcoat it or hold your hand. I'll be giving it to you straight, no chaser. There's no room for excuses or self-pity in the world of the alpha male. If you want to succeed, you need to be willing to do whatever it takes, even if it means getting a little dirty and stepping on some toes along the way.

So, are you ready to embark on the journey of a lifetime? Are you ready to put in the work and become the best version of yourself? Are you ready to take your place among the ranks of the true alpha males?

If the answer is yes, then let's get f***ing started.

1.2 Defining masculinity and the true meaning of being an alpha male

Listen up, you weak-ass, excuse-making losers. It's time to face the facts: society has turned men into pussies. We're living in a world full of betas, who are content to live mediocre lives and never reach their full potential. But that's not you, right? You're here because you want to be a true f***ing alpha male – the kind of man who doesn't give a single f*** about what anyone else thinks.

So, what does it mean to be an alpha male? Some people think it's all about being a dick to everyone around you, but that's not the whole story. Being an alpha male is about being a leader, a fighter, and a man who takes charge of his own life. It's about standing tall in the face of adversity and never backing down. It's about being the kind of man that other men respect and women desire.

The first thing you need to understand is that masculinity isn't some antiquated concept that we should throw away. Sure, there are plenty of guys out there who use it as an excuse to be assholes, but that's not what real masculinity is about. Real masculinity is about strength, honor, and integrity. It's about being a protector and a provider. It's about embracing your role as a man and not shying away from it.

Now, I know what you're thinking: "But Tate, isn't that just some outdated idea of what a man should be?" F*** no. Look around you – the world is full of weak, miserable men who have no idea who they are or what they're capable of. They're slaves to the matrix mindset, just going through the motions and never taking control of their own lives. That's not the kind of man you want to be, is it?

So how do you become an alpha male who doesn't give a f***? It starts with your mindset. You need to get rid of all that self-doubt and insecurity that's been holding you back. You need to start believing in yourself and your ability to overcome any obstacle that comes your way. It's about having the mental fortitude to stare down your fears and crush them beneath your boot.

But it's not just about being tough. An alpha male is also a man of principle. He knows what he stands for and isn't afraid to fight for it, no matter the cost. He's not swayed by the opinions of others, because he knows that true power comes from within.

In this book, I'm going to teach you how to become that kind of man – the kind of man who doesn't give a f*** about what anyone else thinks. We'll dive into the world of masculinity, leadership, and fighting, and I'll share my own experiences as a four-time kickboxing world champion and successful entrepreneur.

But be warned: this journey isn't for the faint of heart. You're going to have to face some harsh truths about yourself and the world around you. You're going to have to push yourself harder than you ever thought possible. But if you're willing to do the work, I promise you one thing: you'll come out the other side as a true alpha male who doesn't give a single f***. And trust me, there's no better feeling in the world.

Chapter 2

The Alpha Male Mindset and Emotional Intelligence

2.1 Developing confidence, self-assurance, resilience, and charisma

Alright, so you've decided to become an alpha male who doesn't give a fuck. Good for you. But that means you need to start working on your confidence, self-assurance, resilience, and charisma. These are the qualities that will set you apart from the rest of the sheep and help you take control of your life.

Let's start with confidence. Confidence is the foundation upon which everything else is built. Without it, you'll never be able to face your fears, take risks, or stand up for yourself. The problem is, most guys have no idea how to build their confidence. They think it's something you're either born with or not. But that's bullshit. Confidence can be developed, just like any other skill.

So how do you build your confidence? The first step is to stop giving a fuck about what other people think. Most guys are so worried about being judged or rejected that they never take any risks or put themselves out there. That's not how an alpha male operates. An alpha male knows that the only opinion that truly matters is his own. So, stop worrying about what other people think and start focusing on what you want.

Next, you need to start taking action. Confidence isn't something you can just think your way into – you need to prove to yourself that you're capable of overcoming obstacles and achieving your goals. Set small, achievable targets and work your way up. Every time you succeed, your confidence will grow. And even when you fail, you'll learn valuable lessons that will make you stronger and more resilient.

Now let's talk about self-assurance. Self-assurance is about knowing your worth and being comfortable with who you are. It's about owning your strengths and weaknesses and not letting anyone else define you. To develop self-assurance, you need to start by getting to know yourself better. Spend some time reflecting on your values, your goals, and your passions. Once you have a clear understanding of who you are and what you stand for, it'll be much easier to project self-assurance to the world.

Resilience is another crucial quality for any alpha male. Life is full of setbacks and obstacles, but an alpha male doesn't let that stop him. Instead, he learns from his mistakes and keeps pushing forward, no matter how tough things get. To develop resilience, you need to start embracing adversity. Stop running away from challenges and start facing them head-on. The more you do this, the stronger and more resilient you'll become.

Finally, we have charisma. Charisma is the secret sauce that makes people want to follow you, listen to you, and be around you. It's a combination of confidence, charm, and genuine interest in others. To develop charisma, you need to work on your communication skills. Learn how to be a good listener, ask engaging questions, and make people feel valued and appreciated. At the same time, practice being assertive and expressing your own opinions and ideas. When you can balance these two aspects, you'll be well on your way to becoming a charismatic leader.

In this chapter, we've covered the essential qualities you need to develop in order to become a true alpha male who doesn't give a fuck: confidence, self-assurance, resilience, and charisma. But remember, developing these qualities takes time and effort. It's not going to happen overnight. You need to be willing to put in the work, face your fears, and keep pushing yourself to new heights. If you can do that, there's no limit to what you can achieve as an alpha male who doesn't give a shit.

2.2 Mastering the art of communication and body language

Alright, you've got your confidence, self-assurance, resilience, and charisma on lock. Now it's time to work on another crucial aspect of being an alpha male: mastering the art of communication and body language. Why is this important? Because communication is the key to building strong relationships, influencing people, and getting what you want in life. And body language is a huge part of that.

First, let's talk about verbal communication. As an alpha male, you need to be able to express yourself clearly and assertively. This means being direct, concise, and to the point. Don't beat around the bush or try to sugarcoat things – people respect honesty, even if it's a little brutal. And don't be afraid to stand up for yourself and your opinions.

Remember, an alpha male doesn't give a fuck about what other people think.

But communication isn't just about talking – it's also about listening. Too many guys make the mistake of dominating the conversation and not giving others a chance to speak. That's not how an alpha male operates. A true alpha male knows the value of active listening and engaging with others. He asks questions, shows genuine interest, and makes people feel heard and understood.

Now let's dive into body language. Your body language speaks volumes about who you are and how you feel, even if you're not saying a word. As an alpha male, you need to be aware of the signals you're sending and make sure they align with the image you want to project.

Start with your posture. Stand tall, with your shoulders back and your chest out. This not only makes you look more confident and powerful, but it also helps you feel that way too. Make sure you maintain eye contact when you're speaking to someone – this shows that you're engaged and interested in what they have to say. But don't stare them down like a psycho – that's just creepy.

Another important aspect of body language is your facial expressions. Learn to control your emotions and project the image you want. If you're trying to be friendly and approachable, smile and maintain a relaxed expression. If you're going for a more dominant and assertive vibe, keep your face neutral and maintain a strong gaze.

Don't forget about your gestures, either. Use your hands and arms to emphasize your points and express yourself. Just don't overdo it – flailing your arms around like a madman will only make you look ridiculous. Keep your movements deliberate and controlled.

Lastly, be aware of the body language of others. Learn to read the subtle cues people give off and adjust your approach accordingly. If someone seems uncomfortable or defensive, try to put them at ease by matching their body language and mirroring their movements. If they're open and engaged, feel free to be more assertive and take control of the conversation.

In this chapter, we've covered the importance of mastering the art of communication and body language for the alpha male who doesn't give a damn. By honing your verbal and non-verbal communication skills, you'll be able to influence people, build powerful relationships, and command respect from those around you.

Remember, though, that becoming a master of communication and body language takes time and practice. You're not going to become a smooth-talking, body language-reading machine overnight. But with dedication and effort, you'll be well on your way to becoming the kind of alpha male who doesn't give a lousy fuck and can navigate any social situation with ease.

Chapter 3

Physical Fitness, Strength, and Self-Defense

3.1 Staying in shape and maintaining a healthy body

Alright, you lazy dudes, it's time to get real about physical fitness, strength, and self-defense. This isn't just about looking good in the mirror, although that's a nice side effect. It's about being a strong, capable man who can protect himself and the people he cares about. So let's get into it.

First things first: you need to stay in shape. And I'm not talking about some pansy-ass cardio routine where you jog on the treadmill for 20 minutes and call it a day. I'm talking about a hardcore, full-body workout that will push you to your limits and make you feel like you're going to die. Why? Because that's what it takes to be an alpha male.

Now, I know what you're thinking: "Tate, I don't have time to work out for hours every day." Well, guess what? Neither do I. But I still find the time to get my ass to the gym and train like a beast. Why? Because it's a fucking priority. If you want to be a true alpha male, you need to make fitness a non-negotiable part of your life.

And don't even get me started on diet. If you're stuffing your face with processed crap and washing it down with soda, you're never going to get the body you want. You need to be eating clean, whole foods – lean meats, vegetables, and healthy fats. Cut out the sugar and processed garbage, and watch your body transform.

But staying in shape isn't just about looking good – it's about being strong and powerful. That's why you need to be lifting heavy weights and focusing on compound exercises like squats, deadlifts, and bench presses. These are the exercises that will build the most muscle and make you feel like a fucking superhero.

And speaking of superheroes, let's talk about self-defense. Because there's no point in being an alpha male who doesn't give a fuck if you can't protect yourself or the people you care about. That's why you need to learn some form of martial arts or combat sports – whether it's boxing, Muay Thai, Brazilian Jiu-Jitsu, or something else entirely.

Now, I know what you're thinking: "But Tate, I don't want to get punched in the face or choked out." Well, too fucking bad. Life is tough, and if you want to be a true alpha male, you need to be able to handle the rough stuff. Besides, there's nothing more exhilarating than stepping into the ring or onto the mats and testing your skills against another human being.

So, how do you get started with all of this? It's simple: find a gym or martial arts school near you and sign up for classes. Don't worry about being the weakest or least skilled person in the room – everyone starts somewhere. Just show up, work hard, and stay consistent. Eventually, you'll start to see progress, and your confidence will skyrocket.

In conclusion, if you want to be an alpha male who doesn't give a shit, you need to focus on physical fitness, strength, and self-defense. Staying in shape and maintaining a healthy body is crucial for building the mental toughness and discipline required to be a true alpha male. And learning how to fight is an essential skill for any man who wants to be able to protect himself and his loved ones.

So, what are you waiting for? Stop making excuses and start taking action. Get your ass to the gym, clean up your diet, and start learning how to throw a punch or execute a submission. Remember, being an alpha male who doesn't give a shit is about more than just talking the talk – you need to walk the walk as well.

And let me tell you something: the journey is worth it. There's nothing more satisfying than looking in the mirror and seeing the physical embodiment of your hard work and discipline. And when you're able to stand up for yourself and protect the people you care about, you'll know that you've truly become an alpha male who doesn't give a fuck.

So stop reading this and start taking action. The sooner you begin, the sooner you'll be able to reap the rewards of your efforts. And trust me, once you start seeing results, you'll never want to go back to being a weak, pathetic version of yourself ever again.

Now go out there and show the world what it means to be an alpha male who doesn't give a fuck. And remember: no matter how hard it gets, no matter how much it hurts, keep pushing forward. Because that's what true alpha males do – they rise to the challenge and conquer it, no matter the odds.

I believe in you, and I know you can do this. So let's fucking go.

3.2 Learning self-defense techniques and defending yourself and others

Alright, you weak-ass motherfuckers, it's time to step up your game and learn how to defend yourself and the people you care about. No alpha male worth his salt is going to stand around like a little bitch while someone tries to harm him or his loved ones. So let's talk about learning self-defense techniques and getting some real skills under your belt.

First off, you need to find a martial art or combat sport that suits your personality and interests. There's no one-size-fits-all answer here – some people are drawn to the striking techniques of boxing or Muay Thai, while others prefer the grappling and submission skills of Brazilian Jiu-Jitsu or wrestling. The key is to find something that you're passionate about, because that's what's going to keep you motivated and focused.

Now, I'm not saying you have to become the next Bruce Lee or Conor McGregor. But you do need to be competent enough to handle yourself in a physical confrontation. And that means putting in the hours and learning from the best. Find a reputable gym or martial arts school, and commit to training consistently. Remember, Rome wasn't built in a day – and neither are badass fighters.

When it comes to self-defense, one of the most important things you need to understand is situational awareness. You've got to be constantly scanning your environment, looking for potential threats or danger. Because the best way to defend yourself is to avoid a fight in the first place. Trust your instincts and pay attention to your surroundings – they'll often give you the early warning signs you need to stay safe.

But sometimes, despite your best efforts, you'll find yourself in a situation where you have to throw down. And when that happens, you need to be ready to fucking go. That means knowing how to strike effectively, how to take someone down, and how to escape from a bad position. It also means having the mental fortitude to stay calm and focused under pressure – because panicking is only going to get you hurt.

Now, let's talk about defending others. Because being an alpha male who doesn't give a shot isn't just about taking care of yourself – it's about looking out for the people you care about, too. Whether it's your family, your friends, or your girl, you need to be ready and willing to step up and protect them if shit goes down.

This means being aware of their safety and well-being, and intervening if you see them in danger. It also means being prepared to put yourself on the line for them – because that's what true alpha males do. They don't run away or hide when things get tough; they face the danger head-on and deal with it, no matter the cost.

In conclusion, learning self-defense techniques and being able to defend yourself and others is a crucial aspect of being an alpha male who doesn't give a fuck. It's about being strong, capable, and confident in your abilities – and using those abilities to protect the people you care about. So find a martial art or combat sport that appeals to you, and start training like a motherfucking warrior.

And remember: the journey to becoming a true alpha male is a long and challenging one. But it's worth it – because there's no greater feeling than knowing you have the skills and the courage to stand up and fight when it matters most.

Now go out there and show the world what it means to be an alpha male who doesn't give a fuck. Train hard, stay focused, and never back down from a challenge. And to give you a little inspiration, let me share some stories from my own kickboxing career.

Back when I was still a young, hungry fighter, I entered a tournament that was way above my skill level. I was up against guys who had been training for years, and I knew I was in for a tough time. But instead of backing down or doubting myself, I decided to fucking go for it – because that's what alpha males do.

In my first fight, I was up against a guy who had a serious reputation for knocking people out. I remember stepping into the ring, looking him dead in the eye, and thinking, "Fuck it, let's do this." The bell rang, and we went at it like two wild animals. I took some heavy shots, but I kept pushing forward, refusing to give up. And in the end, I landed a brutal combination that sent him crashing to the canvas.

That victory taught me something important: when you're willing to face your fears and go toe-to-toe with a tough opponent, you can accomplish amazing things. And that lesson has stuck with me throughout my entire career, both in and out of the ring.

Another memorable moment from my kickboxing days came when I was fighting for a championship title. The stakes were high, and I knew I couldn't afford to make any mistakes. So I trained like a motherfucking demon, pushing my body and mind to their absolute limits.

On the night of the fight, I stepped into the ring feeling like a goddamn superhero. My opponent was strong and skilled, but I knew I had done everything in my power to prepare for this moment. The fight was a brutal, back-and-forth battle, with both of us giving it everything we had.

But in the final round, I dug deep and found a reserve of strength I didn't even know I had. I unleashed a flurry of punches and kicks, overwhelming my opponent and securing the victory – and the championship belt.

These experiences from my kickboxing career have shaped the man I am today – and they're a big part of why I'm so passionate about teaching others the importance of physical fitness, strength, and self-defense. Because I know firsthand what it takes to face your fears, overcome adversity, and emerge victorious.

So let these stories inspire you to become the best version of yourself – an alpha male who doesn't give a fuck. Embrace the challenges, push through the pain, and never, ever give up on your quest for greatness.

Chapter 4

Dressing for Success and Personal Style

4.1 Creating an alpha male wardrobe

Listen up, you style-challenged motherfuckerers: it's time to step your game up and create a wardrobe that reflects your status as an alpha male. I'm not saying you have to dress like a fashion model or spend a fortune on designer clothes, but you do need to pay attention to your appearance and make sure you're sending the right message to the world.

First things first: you need to invest in some high-quality, well-fitting clothes. There's nothing worse than a dude walking around in a baggy, ill-fitting suit or jeans that are two sizes too big. You don't have to break the bank, but you should be willing to spend a little extra to get clothes that fit you properly and are made from good materials.

Next, let's talk about the basics. Every alpha male's wardrobe should include a few essential items:

1 A killer suit: A sharp, well-tailored suit is a must for any alpha male. You never know when you'll need to attend a business meeting or a fancy event, and you want to make sure you're looking your best. Invest in at least one high-quality suit that fits you like a glove.

2 A badass leather jacket: I don't care who you are – every man looks cooler in a leather jacket. It's a timeless piece that adds an edge to any outfit and makes you look like a fucking rockstar.

3 High-quality denim: A great pair of jeans is a staple in any alpha male's wardrobe. Find a brand and fit that works for your body type, and don't be afraid to spend a little extra for a pair that will last.

4 Stylish, versatile shoes: You don't need a closet full of shoes, but you should have a few go-to pairs for different occasions. Invest in some classic, well-made dress shoes for formal events, a pair of stylish sneakers for casual wear, and some boots for when you need to kick some ass.

5 Accessories that make a statement: A nice watch, a killer pair of sunglasses, and a few other carefully chosen accessories can take your outfit to the next

level. Don't go overboard, but do choose pieces that reflect your personality and make a statement.

Now that you've got the basics covered, it's time to develop your personal style. This is where you can really let your inner alpha male shine. Are you a badass biker type who loves leather and chains? Or maybe you're more of a suave, sophisticated gentleman who prefers tailored suits and designer labels? Whatever your vibe, own it and wear it with confidence.

A big part of developing your personal style is experimenting with different looks and finding what works for you. Don't be afraid to take risks or try new things – that's how you'll discover your true style and learn how to rock it like a boss.

Finally, remember that your appearance is just one part of the equation. Being an alpha male who doesn't give a fuck is about more than just looking good – it's about feeling good, too. So make sure you're taking care of your body, staying in shape, and maintaining a healthy lifestyle. Because when you feel like a million bucks, you'll look like it, too.

In conclusion, creating an alpha male wardrobe is all about finding high-quality, well-fitting clothes that reflect your personal style and make you feel like the badass you are. Invest in the essentials, take risks, and own your look with confidence. And remember: being an alpha male who doesn't give a fuck isn't just about dressing the part – it's about living the part, too.

Let me give you an example from my own life. Back when I was starting to make a name for myself, I knew that my appearance mattered. People judge you based on how you look, and I wasn't going to let them think I was just another average dude. So I started dressing like the alpha male I knew I was – and it made a huge difference.

I'd walk into a room wearing a perfectly tailored suit or rocking my favorite leather jacket, and people would notice. I could see the respect in their eyes and feel the attention shift to me. That's the power of dressing like an alpha male – it commands respect and sets you apart from the crowd.

But it wasn't just about the clothes. I also made sure I was taking care of myself physically – working out, eating right, and staying in peak condition. Because when you look good, you feel good – and when you feel good, you radiate confidence and power.

So if you want to become an alpha male who doesn't give a fuck, start by upgrading your wardrobe and developing your personal style. Invest in high-quality clothes that fit you well and make you feel like the badass you are. Experiment with different looks, take risks, and own your style with confidence.

And don't forget to focus on the bigger picture, too. Being an alpha male isn't just about dressing the part – it's about living the part, too. So make sure you're taking care of your body, staying in shape, and maintaining a healthy lifestyle. Because when you look and feel like a million bucks, people will treat you like it, too.

Now get out there and show the world what it means to be an alpha male. Make a statement with your style, own your confidence, and never let anyone tell you that you can't achieve greatness. Because when you dress for success and live like a true alpha male, the world is yours for the taking.

4.2 The significance of grooming and personal style

Alright, you grooming legends, it's time to talk about something that most guys overlook but is absolutely crucial to being an alpha male who doesn't give a fuck: grooming and personal style. You might have the best wardrobe in the world, but if you're walking around with a scraggly beard, greasy hair, and bad breath, you're still gonna look like a fucking bum.

Let's start with the basics: hygiene. I shouldn't have to say this, but you'd be surprised how many dudes neglect the simple act of showering and brushing their teeth. You want to be an alpha male? Start by taking care of yourself and keeping clean. No one respects a man who smells like shit and looks like he just crawled out of a dumpster.

Now that we've got the basics out of the way, let's talk about grooming. This is where the real magic happens, and it's what separates the alpha males from the beta bitches. You need to take care of your hair, your beard (if you have one), and your skin. Get regular haircuts, trim your beard, and for the love of all things holy, moisturize your face. Trust me, it makes a difference.

When it comes to hair, find a style that works for you and stick with it. This doesn't mean you can't change things up, but it does mean that you should have a signature look that reflects your personality and your status as an alpha male. If you're not sure where to start, talk to a good barber or hairstylist – they'll be able to give you some guidance.

Now let's talk about personal style. This goes beyond just your clothes – it's about how you present yourself to the world. It's the way you walk, the way you talk, and the way you carry yourself. An alpha male who doesn't give a f*** is confident, self-assured, and in control. He knows what he wants, and he isn't afraid to go after it.

This doesn't mean you need to be an arrogant prick – but it does mean you need to stand up for yourself and your beliefs. If someone challenges you, don't back down – stand your ground and show them who's boss. And if you see someone being disrespected, step in and defend them. That's what a real alpha male does.

In my own life, I've always made a point of taking care of my appearance and presenting myself with confidence. I know that when I walk into a room, people are going to judge me based on how I look – and I want to make sure they're judging me as the fucking boss I am.

So, in conclusion, being an alpha male who doesn't give a fuck isn't just about dressing well and having a killer wardrobe – it's about taking care of yourself, grooming properly, and presenting yourself with confidence and swagger. If you want to command respect and be seen as a true leader, you need to pay attention to every aspect of your appearance and personal style.

Now get out there and show the world what it means to be an alpha male who doesn't give a fuck. Be confident, be bold, and never let anyone tell you that you can't achieve greatness. Because when you look and feel like a million bucks, you'll be unstoppable.

Chapter 5

Career, Financial Mastery, and Leadership

5.1 Cultivating discipline, ambition, and leadership skills

Alright, you fucking legends, let's cut through the bullshit and get down to business. You want to be an alpha male who doesn't give a fuck? Then you need to cultivate discipline, ambition, and leadership skills that'll put you on top of the world. And I'm here to show you exactly how to do that, so buckle up, losers, and pay attention.

Let's start with discipline. You think success just falls into your lap? Hell no. It takes hard work, dedication, and the willingness to push through the pain when every fiber of your being wants to give up. I'll tell you right now, if you're not disciplined, you're never gonna make it in this world. You'll just be another broke loser living in his mom's basement, whining about how life isn't fair.

So how do you build discipline? By setting goals and sticking to them, no matter what. You want to get in shape? Get your ass to the gym every day. You want to build a business? Put in the hours and make it happen. No excuses, no bullshit. That's what separates the winners from the losers in this world.

Now let's talk about ambition. You think I got where I am today by being a lazy fuck who's satisfied with mediocrity? Hell no. I'm always pushing myself to achieve more, to be better, to conquer new challenges. And that's what you need to do if you want to be an alpha male who doesn't give a fuck.

I've seen too many guys with potential waste their lives because they're afraid to dream big. They're scared of failure, of rejection, of looking stupid. But let me tell you something – the only thing that's truly stupid is living a life filled with regret because you never had the balls to go after what you really wanted.

Finally, let's talk about leadership. You want to be an alpha male? Then you need to be a fucking leader. That means taking charge, making decisions, and commanding respect. But it also means being a mentor, a role model, and someone who's willing to help others succeed.

In my life, I've always stepped up to be a leader, whether it was in kickboxing, in business, or in my personal relationships. I've never been afraid to take charge, and I've never been afraid to make the tough calls. And you know what? People respect that. They follow me because they know I'll lead them to success.

So, to all you wannabe alpha males out there, it's time to step up your game. Cultivate discipline, ambition, and leadership skills, and watch as your life transforms before your eyes. Stop being a broke loser who whines about how hard life is, and start being a fucking winner who goes out and takes what he wants.

Remember, life doesn't reward the weak, the timid, or the lazy. It rewards those who are bold, determined, and relentless in their pursuit of greatness. So, are you gonna be a loser, or are you gonna be an alpha male who doesn't give a fuck? The choice is yours.

5.2 Building wealth and maintaining financial independence

Alright, you fucking legends, it's time to talk about something that too many people are afraid to discuss: money. You want to be an alpha male that doesn't give a fuck? Then you need to build wealth and achieve financial independence. There's no room for broke losers in this lifestyle, so listen up and take notes.

First off, let me tell you something: money is power. It gives you the freedom to do what you want, when you want, and with whom you want. I didn't get to where I am today by being a broke, pathetic loser. No, I built my empire, and I continue to expand it every day.

So how do you build wealth? It starts with having a solid plan and a fucking work ethic that puts everyone else to shame. You can't be lazy and expect to make money – it just doesn't work that way. You have to hustle, grind, and put in the hours to make your dreams a reality.

Next, you need to invest. You think I got rich by stashing my money in a savings account? Fuck no. I invested in businesses, real estate, stocks, and more. And guess what? It paid off. Learn about different investment strategies and find the ones that work for you. The key is to diversify your portfolio and let your money work for you while you sleep.

Now, let's talk about financial independence. This isn't just about having a shit ton of money in the bank – it's about being able to live life on your terms without worrying about how you're going to pay your bills. You want to travel the world? Go for it. You want to buy a fucking Lamborghini? Do it. When you're financially independent, you have the power to make those decisions without fear or hesitation.

But here's the thing: financial independence isn't just handed to you. You have to work for it, and you have to be disciplined with your money. That means living within your means, saving and investing consistently, and always looking for new opportunities to grow your wealth.

And for fuck's sake, don't be one of those idiots who blows all their money on stupid shit like designer clothes and overpriced bottles at the club. That's a surefire way to end up broke and miserable. Instead, invest in yourself and your future. Spend your money on things that will help you grow as a person and as an alpha male.

Finally, let me share a little secret with you: the truly wealthy don't give a fuck what other people think about them. They don't need to prove anything to anyone because they know their worth. They don't waste time trying to impress people with their money – they just live life to the fullest and enjoy the fruits of their labor.

So, if you want to be an alpha male that doesn't give a fuck, it's time to start building wealth and achieving financial independence. Get your ass in gear, work hard, invest smart, and live life on your terms. The world is yours for the taking – are you going to seize it, or are you going to let it slip through your fingers like a broke loser?

The choice is yours, gentlemen. Make it a good one.

Chapter 6

The Alpha Male in Relationships and Friendships

6.1 Attracting and maintaining healthy relationships with women

Listen up, you fucking losers, because we're about to dive into one of the most important aspects of being an alpha male that doesn't give a fuck: attracting and maintaining healthy relationships with women.

Now, I know what you're thinking: "Andrew, I'm already a smooth-talking, charming motherfucker. I don't need any help with the ladies." Well, guess what, buddy? You're fucking wrong. If you were as good with women as you think, you wouldn't be reading this book, would you?

First things first: if you want to attract high-quality women, you need to be a high-quality man. That means taking care of your body, dressing well, and having your shit together financially. If you don't have your life in order, why the fuck would any woman want to be with you? Get your act together, and the ladies will follow.

Now, let's talk about confidence. Women can smell insecurity from a mile away, and it's a major turn-off. You need to walk into a room like you own the place and make women feel like they'd be lucky to be with you. Fake it 'til you make it, if you have to – eventually, that confidence will become real.

When it comes to conversation, too many guys fuck it up by being boring, predictable, or just plain creepy. Don't be that guy. Instead, be genuinely interested in what the woman has to say, ask engaging questions, and make her laugh. Trust me, a good sense of humor is like catnip to women.

And for fuck's sake, don't be needy or clingy. Women hate that shit. You need to have your own life, your own interests, and your own friends. If you make a woman the center of your universe, she's going to feel suffocated and lose interest fast.

Now, let's talk about maintaining healthy relationships. This is where a lot of guys drop the ball. They think that once they've got a woman, they can just coast and stop putting in effort. That's a surefire way to end up single and miserable.

In a relationship, you need to be the leader. That doesn't mean being a controlling asshole – it means taking charge, making decisions, and being a rock for your woman when she needs you. It also means being emotionally available and willing to communicate openly and honestly about your feelings. Real alpha males aren't afraid to show vulnerability.

And don't forget to keep the romance alive. Surprise your woman with thoughtful gestures, plan exciting dates, and keep the passion burning in the bedroom. A healthy relationship requires ongoing effort and attention, so don't get complacent.

Lastly, let's touch on friendships. A true alpha male surrounds himself with other strong, successful men who share his values and ambitions. You are the company you keep, so if you're hanging out with a bunch of broke losers, it's time to find some new friends. Build a solid support network of like-minded men who will push you to be the best version of yourself.

So there you have it, gents. Attracting and maintaining healthy relationships with women isn't rocket science, but it does require effort, confidence, and a willingness to be vulnerable. Step up, be a leader, and watch as your love life takes off like a fucking rocket.

6.2 Building a supportive network of like-minded men

Listen up, you lazy fuckers. You want to be an alpha male, right? You want to dominate life and have success in every area? Well, guess what? You're not going to do that by hanging around a bunch of losers who don't have any ambition or drive. You need to surround yourself with like-minded men who are just as hungry for success as you are.

You might be thinking, "But Andrew, how the fuck do I find these people?" Don't worry, I've got you covered.

First off, let me tell you a story from my own life. When I started kickboxing, I knew I needed to surround myself with people who were better than me. I sought out training partners who were more skilled and experienced so I could learn from them and become the best. If I had just stuck with the same old crowd, I would never have become the four-time world champion that I am today.

Now, let's get back to building your network. It's not as hard as you might think. Here's what you need to do:

1 Cut out the losers. If you're hanging around with people who are dragging you down or holding you back, it's time to say goodbye. You don't need that kind of negativity in your life.

2 Look for like-minded men in the right places. You're not going to find ambitious, driven people sitting on their couch watching Netflix. Go to events, join clubs, and put yourself in situations where you're likely to meet people who share your goals and values.

3 Be the kind of person you want to attract. If you want to be friends with successful, motivated people, you need to be successful and motivated yourself. Work on yourself, develop your skills, and become the alpha male you want to be. You'll find that like-minded people are naturally drawn to you.

4 Offer value. Nobody wants to hang around with a leech who's always taking but never giving anything in return. Be someone who offers support, encour-

agement, and knowledge to your friends. They'll appreciate it and be more likely to reciprocate.

5 Be selective. You don't need a huge network of friends. In fact, it's better to have a smaller group of close, loyal friends than a large group of acquaintances. Focus on building strong relationships with a few people who really matter.

Remember, you are the average of the five people you spend the most time with. So make sure those people are helping you become the best version of yourself. Don't waste your time on losers and weaklings who will only drag you down. Build a supportive network of like-minded men, and together, you'll all become unstoppable alpha males who don't give a fuck.

Chapter 7

Expanding Your Knowledge and Skills

7.1 The significance of continuous self-improvement

Listen up, you pathetic fuckers. You still want to become a real alpha male, right? Well, guess what? It doesn't happen overnight. You have to continuously work on yourself, learn new shit, and never be satisfied with where you're at. That's the only way you'll become the kind of man who doesn't give a fuck.

I've seen so many losers who think they've "made it" because they've got a decent job, a girlfriend, or a little bit of money in the bank. Let me tell you something – that's not enough. You want to be a real alpha male? You have to keep pushing yourself, keep improving, and never settle for mediocrity.

Here's how you can start your journey of continuous self-improvement:

1 Develop a growth mindset. You need to believe that you can always get better, no matter how good you are right now. I don't give a fuck if you're the best in the world at something – there's always room for improvement.

2 Set goals. Don't just sit around dreaming about the person you want to be. Set specific, measurable goals for yourself and work on them every single day. And when you achieve those goals, set new ones. Never stop pushing yourself to be better.

3 Learn from the best. You think I became a four-time world kickboxing champion by just watching YouTube videos? Fuck no. I sought out the best trainers, the best fighters, and learned from them. Find people who are already at the top of their game and learn from them. It doesn't matter if it's in business, sports, or anything else – there's always someone you can learn from.

4 Stay curious. The world is a fascinating place, and there's always more to learn. Don't get complacent or think you know everything. Stay curious, ask questions, and keep expanding your knowledge.

5 Keep pushing your limits. You'll never know what you're capable of if you don't test yourself. Push

your boundaries, challenge yourself, and take risks. It's the only way you'll truly grow.

Now, you might be thinking, "Andrew, you're a fucking genius. How do you find the time to keep improving yourself?" Well, let me tell you a little secret – I make the time. I prioritize my self-improvement above almost everything else. I don't waste my time on stupid shit like watching TV or playing video games. I read, I train, and I work on my businesses.

So, if you want to become an alpha male who doesn't give a fuck, you need to start taking your self-improvement seriously. Stop hanging out with losers who are content with mediocrity. Surround yourself with winners who are committed to growth and success. And never, ever be satisfied with where you're at.

Remember, the world doesn't give a fuck about you. It's up to you to make something of yourself, and the only way to do that is through continuous self-improvement. So get off your lazy ass, start working on yourself, and become the alpha male you were born to be.

7.2 Learning from the success of others

You know what's the difference between an alpha male and a broke loser? The alpha male learns from the success of others, while the broke loser sits around feeling sorry for himself, blaming everyone else for his failures. If you want to be an alpha male that doesn't give a fuck, you need to start learning from the success of others.

Listen up, because I'm about to share some hard-hitting truths that will transform your life, if you have the balls to apply them.

First things first, you've got to stop being a hater. I've seen so many fucking losers who spend their time hating on successful people, instead of learning from them. These are the same morons who claim that successful people are "lucky" or that they "cheated" their way to the top. Newsflash, dipshit: Success doesn't come from luck or cheating. It comes from hard work, discipline, and learning from the people who've already made it.

So, how do you learn from the success of others? Here's a step-by-step guide:

1. Find role models. You need to identify successful people in your field or area of interest. It doesn't matter if they're billionaires, athletes, or world-class artists – just find someone who's achieved the level of success you aspire to.

2. Study their lives. Read their biographies, watch interviews, and learn everything you can about their journey to success. Find out what habits, mindsets, and strategies helped them achieve their goals.

3. Emulate their success. Adopt the habits, mindsets, and strategies that worked for your role models. If they wake up at 5 am every day, you wake up at 5 am. If they read a book a week, you read a book a week. If they spend two hours a day working on their craft, you spend two hours a day working on your craft.

4. Network with successful people. This one's a game-changer. If you surround yourself with successful people, their success will rub off on you. Attend conferences, join clubs, and do whatever it takes to get in the same room as the people you admire.

5. Learn from their failures. It's not just about copying their successes; you need to learn from their mistakes as well. Find out what they did wrong and avoid making the same errors.

Now, let me tell you a little story from my own life. When I started my journey to become a world-class kickboxer, I didn't just waltz into a gym and start punching bags. No, I sought out the best trainers and fighters I could find, and I learned from them. I studied their techniques, their training methods, and their mindset. And you know what? It fucking worked. I became a four-time world kickboxing champion.

The same principle applies to every aspect of your life. Want to be a successful entrepreneur? Learn from the best business minds out there. Want to have an amazing physique? Learn from top fitness trainers and bodybuilders. Stop being a fucking know-it-all, and start learning from the people who've actually achieved what you want to achieve.

So, there you have it. If you want to be an alpha male that doesn't give a fuck, start learning from the success of others. It's the fastest way to level up your life and become the kind of man that everyone admires and respects. And remember: the only person holding you back is yourself. Get out of your own way, and start learning from the best.

Chapter 8

The Art of Seduction and Female Psychology

8.1 Approaching and attracting women with confidence

Listen up, motherfuckers. I'm about to drop some serious knowledge on you about the art of approaching and attracting women with confidence. This is some top-shelf shit that has helped me pull some of the most beautiful women you've ever seen. So grab a pen and paper, and get ready to take notes.

First of all, let's clear one thing up: if you're not confident when you approach a woman, you're fucked. Women can smell insecurity from a mile away, and they're not attracted to that weak shit. So if you want to be an alpha male that doesn't give a fuck, you need to learn how to approach women with confidence.

How do you do that? Here are my tried-and-tested tips:

1 Embrace rejection. You're going to get rejected. A lot. It's part of the game. Instead of letting rejection destroy your confidence, use it as a learning experience. Every rejection is an opportunity to improve your approach, so don't be afraid to fail.

2 Get comfortable with being uncomfortable. Approaching women can be scary as fuck, but you need to push through that fear. The more you do it, the more comfortable you'll become, and the more confident you'll appear.

3 Don't give a fuck. I can't stress this enough: the less you care about the outcome, the more confident you'll be. If you approach a woman with the mindset that you don't give a fuck if she rejects you, your confidence will skyrocket.

4 Body language is key. Stand tall, make eye contact, and own your space. A confident posture will make you more attractive to women and will also make you feel more confident.

5 Be direct. Don't beat around the bush or try to be clever. Just walk up to her, introduce yourself, and tell her you think she's attractive. Women appreciate

a man who knows what he wants and isn't afraid to go after it.

Now, let me share a personal story to illustrate how confidence can make all the difference when it comes to approaching women. A few years ago, I was at a party in Bucharest. The place was packed with beautiful women, and I had my eye on one in particular.

Instead of hesitating or worrying about what to say, I walked straight up to her, looked her in the eye, and said, "I'm Andrew Tate. I saw you from across the room, and I had to come and introduce myself. You're absolutely stunning."

She was taken aback by my directness, but you know what? She loved it. We spent the rest of the night talking, and I ended up taking her home. Confidence, my friends, is the ultimate aphrodisiac.

To sum it up, if you want to be an alpha male that doesn't give a fuck, you need to learn how to approach and attract women with confidence. Embrace rejection, get comfortable with being uncomfortable, don't give a fuck about the outcome, master your body language, and be direct. Do these things, and you'll be drowning in beautiful women in no time.

Now get out there and start putting this knowledge to work. The world needs more alpha males who aren't afraid to go after what they want. Don't let fear and insecurity hold you back. Be the man you were born to be, and start living the life you deserve.

8.2 Understanding female psychology

Alright, you fucking degenerates. Listen up, because I'm about to drop some knowledge on the mysterious world of female psychology. Once you understand how women think, you'll be able to seduce them like a pro. So buckle up and get ready to learn some shit.

First off, let's get one thing straight: women are not men. They think differently, they feel differently, and they respond to shit differently. If you want to be successful with women, you need to stop projecting your own male perspective onto them.

Now, here's what you need to know about female psychology:

1 Emotions are king. Women are emotional creatures, and they respond to emotions more than

logic. If you can make a woman feel something, you're halfway to seducing her. Focus on creating an emotional connection and stirring up positive emotions in her.

2 Women crave validation. This is a harsh truth, but most women are insecure as fuck. They want to feel desired and appreciated. If you can make a woman feel like she's the most beautiful and interesting woman in the room, she'll be eating out of your hand.

3 The power of mystery. Women are attracted to men who are intriguing and mysterious. If you can keep her guessing and maintain an air of mystery, she'll be hooked. Don't reveal too much about yourself too soon. Let her discover your secrets bit by bit.

4 Social proof matters. Women are more likely to be attracted to men who are popular and respected by others. If you have a strong social circle and other women find you attractive, the woman you're pursuing will be more likely to see you as a catch.

5 The push-pull dynamic. Women are drawn to men who are confident and assertive, but they also want to feel like they've earned your attention. You need to strike a balance between showing interest

and pulling away. Keep her on her toes by occasionally withdrawing your attention and making her work for it.

Now, let me share an anecdote to illustrate the power of understanding female psychology. I was at a club in London, and I spotted a gorgeous woman surrounded by a group of guys. Most men would be intimidated by that situation, but not me. I knew exactly how to use female psychology to my advantage.

I approached the group and immediately focused my attention on her. I asked her about her life and her passions, creating an emotional connection while also validating her. I made her feel like she was the most important person in the room, and the other guys quickly faded into the background.

Throughout the night, I maintained an air of mystery and kept her guessing about my intentions. I also made a point of talking to other women and demonstrating my social proof. Finally, I employed the push-pull dynamic, occasionally withdrawing my attention and making her work to regain it.

By the end of the night, she was hooked. She couldn't resist the psychological cocktail I'd served her, and I ended up taking her home. That, my friends, is the power of understanding female psychology.

In conclusion, if you want to be an alpha male that doesn't give a fuck, you need to understand female psychology. Focus on emotions, provide validation, maintain mystery, demonstrate social proof, and use the push-pull dynamic. Once you master these principles, you'll have women lining up to be with you.

Now go out there and put this knowledge to the test. Remember, the world needs more alpha males who know how to handle women. Don't let your own ignorance hold you back. Understand female psychology, and become the man that every woman wants.

Chapter 9

Creating a Powerful Social Circle and Finding Your Passion

9.1 Networking with successful people and discovering fulfilling hobbies

Listen up, motherfuckers. If you want to be a true alpha male, you need to surround yourself with successful people and fill your life with hobbies that you're genuinely passionate about. No one wants to be friends with a loser who spends his days jerking off and playing video games. It's time to level up your social life and find some shit that makes you excited to wake up in the morning.

First, let's talk about networking with successful people. You know that old saying, "You are the average of the five people you spend the most time with"? Well, it's fucking true. If you hang around a bunch of broke, miserable losers, you'll end up becoming one too. So ditch those deadweights and start connecting with people who are actually going somewhere in life.

Here are some tips on networking like a boss:

1 Attend events and conferences. Get your ass off the couch and go to places where successful people gather. This could be industry conferences, networking events, or even high-end clubs and bars. Just make sure you're putting yourself in a position to meet the kind of people you want to associate with.

2 Be genuinely interested in others. When you meet someone new, make it your mission to learn as much as you can about them. Ask questions, listen to their stories, and show genuine interest in their lives. People love talking about themselves, and they'll be more likely to remember you if you make them feel heard.

3 Offer value. Don't be a leech who's only looking to take from others. Find ways to provide value to the people you meet, whether it's by sharing your knowledge, offering a connection, or just being a supportive friend. The more value you bring to the table, the more people will want to be around you.

Now let's talk about finding fulfilling hobbies. If all you do is work, eat, sleep, and repeat, you're gonna burn out and become a boring-ass motherfucker.

You need to find activities that make you excited and bring joy to your life.

Here are some tips on discovering your passions:

1 Experiment with different activities. You won't know if you enjoy something until you try it. So go out and try a bunch of different shit – join a sports team, take a cooking class, learn a musical instrument, or start painting. You never know what might ignite your passion.

2 Don't be afraid to fail. Not every hobby you try will be a home run, and that's okay. The point is to find something that you enjoy and can become skilled at over time. So don't worry if you suck at first – embrace the learning process and keep pushing forward.

3 Make it social. Hobbies are more fun when you share them with others. Join clubs or groups related to your interests, and you'll not only improve your skills but also expand your social circle.

So there you have it. If you want to be an alpha male who doesn't give a fuck, you need to network with successful people and find hobbies that make you happy. Start attending events, being genuinely interested in others, and offering value. Experiment with different activities, embrace failure, and make your hobbies social.

Remember, life is too short to be a broke, boring loser. Surround yourself with success, fill your life with passion, and watch as your alpha male status skyrockets. Now get the fuck out there and start living your best life.

9.2 The benefits of being well-connected and having diverse interests

Listen up, fuckers. If you think being an alpha male is all about being jacked and banging chicks, you've got it all wrong. Sure, those things are important, but if you really want to be the ultimate alpha male, you need to build a powerful social circle and have diverse interests. Let me break it down for you – here's why it's crucial to be well-connected and have a wide range of hobbies.

First off, being well-connected means you have access to opportunities and resources that the average Joe doesn't. When you know the right people, doors open up for you. Think about it – if you're friends with the CEO of a company, it's a hell of a lot easier to land that high-paying job than if you're just some nobody off the street. So stop being a lazy fuck and start networking like your life depends on it.

Not only will your connections help you in your career, but they can also improve your personal life. Imagine having friends who can get you into exclusive parties or hook you up with discounts at their businesses. When you're well-connected, your life becomes exponentially more enjoyable.

Now let's talk about having diverse interests. If all you do is sit at home and jerk off to porn, you're a boring motherfucker. Nobody wants to be around someone who has nothing interesting to say. By having a variety of hobbies, you become a more well-rounded and intriguing person.

Plus, having diverse interests can also benefit your mental health. Studies have shown that people who engage in a wide range of activities are generally happier and less stressed than those who don't. So, not only will you be more interesting to others, but you'll also feel better about yourself.

Here are some of the key benefits of being well-connected and having diverse interests:

1. Increased opportunities: When you know influential people, they can hook you up with job offers, business deals, and other opportunities that can elevate your status and success.

2. Better social life: Having a powerful social circle means you'll always have people to hang out with, whether it's for a night out on the town or a chill BBQ at your buddy's place.

3. More interesting conversations: With diverse interests, you'll always have something to talk about, making you a captivating conversationalist and drawing people to you like moths to a flame.

4. Personal growth: Pursuing a variety of hobbies forces you to step out of your comfort zone and learn new skills, making you a more well-rounded and adaptable person.

5. Improved mental health: Engaging in diverse activities can reduce stress, boost happiness, and make you feel more fulfilled in life.

Now that you understand the benefits, it's time to get off your lazy ass and start building connections and exploring new interests. Attend networking events, join clubs, and try out different hobbies. Remember, if you want to be an alpha male who doesn't give a fuck, you need to create a powerful social circle and have diverse interests.

So get out there and start living a life that others can only dream of. Embrace your inner alpha, and watch as your life becomes more exciting, fulfilling, and downright badass.

Chapter 10

Conclusion: Leaving a Legacy and the Never-ending Journey

Chapter 11

Lifelong pursuit of self-improvement

Alright, motherfuckers, this is it – the final chapter. If you've made it this far, then congrats, you're not a complete pussy. But guess what? The journey doesn't end here. Being an alpha male who doesn't give a fuck is a lifelong pursuit of self-improvement. You don't just hit a certain level and then coast for the rest of your life. Nah, fuck that. You've got to keep pushing yourself, keep learning, and keep growing. That's what it's all about.

Listen, life is a never-ending game, and if you ain't playing to win, you're just wasting your fucking time. Embracing self-improvement means constantly seeking new ways to grow, evolve, and dominate. It means learning from your failures, not dwelling on them like some pussy-ass brookie.

You think I, TopG, got to where I am today by being complacent? Fuck no. I've faced countless obstacles and setbacks, but I didn't let them break me. I took those experiences and used them to build an empire. I've won world championships, made millions, and traveled the world – all because I refused to accept mediocrity.

So, how do you embrace the lifelong pursuit of self-improvement? Here are some key steps to get you started:

1 Never stop learning: Keep reading books (only the great ones, otherwise skip reading), attending seminars, and learning from others and getting shit done. The more you know, the more powerful you become. Knowledge is fucking power, my friends.

2 Set goals and crush them: Always have a target in mind – something to strive for. Whether it's a new business venture, a fitness goal, or learning a new skill, set a goal and then demolish it. Remember, you're an alpha male who doesn't give a fuck, so act like it.

3 Surround yourself with winners: You're the average of the five people you spend the most time with. So make sure you're hanging out with success-

ful, motivated motherfuckers who are on the same path as you. Losers will only drag you down.

4 Embrace failure: Failure is inevitable, but it's how you handle it that matters. When you fuck up, don't wallow in self-pity. Instead, learn from it and come back stronger. Use failure as fuel to propel you forward.

5 Keep pushing your limits: Don't get comfortable. Comfort is the enemy of progress. Always seek new challenges and push yourself to be better than you were yesterday. That's how you become a true alpha male.

Remember, you're building a legacy. When you're on your deathbed, do you want to look back on a life of mediocrity and regret? Or do you want to know that you lived like a fucking king, conquering every challenge that came your way? I know what I'd choose.

So, my fellow alphas, it's time to embark on the never-ending journey of self-improvement. Keep pushing, keep striving, and never settle for anything less than greatness. This is your life, so make it fucking legendary.

Now go forth and be the alpha male that doesn't give a fuck. Your empire awaits.

. . .

Find more infos at www.cobratate.com

Have You Also Read?

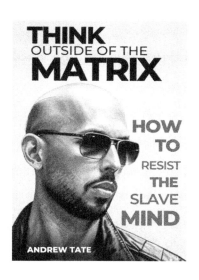

Andrew Tate: Think Outside Of The Matrix - 25 Ways How to Resist the Slave Mind

On   **Amazon:**
www.amazon.com/dp/B0C6WGBZ9C

Book Summary

Andrew Tate reveals deep game-changing principles to help you unlock your potential, reject mediocrity, and challenge societal norms. The book serves as a radical manifesto for anyone who aspires to think independently and live extraordinarily. Immerse yourself in Andrew's 25 provocative insights, and arm yourself with the mindset and tools to shatter the illusions of the Matrix.

<u>Highlights In The Book</u>

- Understanding what the matrix is and why resisting it will lead to greater personal freedom.
- Unleash the power of independent thought and break free from societal constraints.
- Cultivate an unapologetic ambition and audacity to dream big.
- Embrace controversy, challenge status quo, and disrupt conventional practices.
- Learn how to manipulate the Matrix and use societal structures to your advantage.
- Harness the power of solitude for improved clarity and creativity.
- Overcome fear, reject victim mentality, and embrace personal power and responsibility.
- Understand how your perception shapes your reality and learn to reprogram it.

- Master emotional control to prevent emotions from dictating your decisions.
- Develop strategies to outwit the system and turn the game to your advantage.
- Learn to recognize and break free from illusions that limit your potential.

Whom This Book is For

- Individuals tired of societal norms and seeking unconventional paths to success.
- Those yearning to break free from mental slavery and manipulation.
- Aspiring mavericks looking to nurture their rebellious spirit.
- People seeking to challenge authority, resist mass media, and form their own opinions.
- Anyone who aspires to cultivate mental sovereignty and live an extraordinary life.

Printed in Great Britain
by Amazon